YORKSHIRE SPORTING
FACTS & FEATS

RONNIE WHARTON

Dalesman

Dalesman Publishing Company Ltd
Stable Courtyard, Broughton Hall,
Skipton, North Yorkshire BD23 3AZ

First published 2000

Text © Ronnie Wharton

Cartoons by The Silvey-Jex Partnership

A British Library Cataloguing in Publication record
is available for this book

ISBN 1 85568 184-6

Printed by Amadeus Press, Cleckheaton

CONTENTS

FOOTBALL

With the advent of 'mega bucks', TV money and the formation of an elite Premier division containing many of the best players in the world, football has changed. We've seen it move from fighting with other sports for space on the back page of a newspaper to front page headlines when one player has a tattoo done or changes his hairstyle or another has too many drinks in a nightclub.

At one time only a percentage of kids were interested in playing football; now with gross marketing in the media (25 years ago only *players* wore shirts) both genders are hooked on the game and footballers share the same role as pop stars might have done earlier.

It is a far cry from the days when women were let in for nothing until it was revealed how many were attending matches. Even in later years for those who couldn't afford it, clubs would open their gates at half time and I have fond memories of getting in at the boys' gate until I was 21. Clubs were glad of your money.

YORKSHIRE'S FOOTBALL LEAGUE CLUBS

Yorkshire has had a steady average of just over a dozen Football League clubs. There have been casualties along the way particularly in the last few seasons since the non-league pyramid system was extended to the Football League and clubs could be promoted from and relegated to the Conference League. Recent clubs to lose their league status, Doncaster Rovers and Scarborough, can take heart from Halifax Town who rose from the despair of losing over 70 years service by returning in triumph after a few seasons absence.

Barnsley

Formed: 1887
Ground: Oakwell (1887)
Football League: 1898
Previous Name: Barnsley St Peters
Nicknames: The Tykes, Reds

Formed by a chap with the delightful name of Revd Tiverton Preedy, their name changed to Barnsley after one year in the League. The Tykes spent more years in division two than any other team, but two seasons stand out in their history. In 1912 they won the FA Cup with a series of hard-fought displays. (In their 12 matches in the competition they had six 0-0 draws and won five of the others by a goal margin including the final replay when the only goal came in the last minute of extra time.) And in 1998 when managed by Danny Wilson,

Barnsley gained promotion to the Premier to sample the life of one season in the top flight.

Bradford City
Formed: 1903
Ground: Valley Parade (1903)
Football League: 1903
Nicknames: Bantams, Paraders

Though there had been earlier football at the ground and an earlier Bradford City, the present side was elected in 1903 to the Football League without kicking a ball. The ground had previously housed the successful Manningham Rugby team and the FA were presumably keen to establish football in what had been a predominantly rugby area. Inside ten years the club had their first success when they followed the 1908 second division championship with the 1911 FA Cup. Tragedy was to strike in 1985 when the club, celebrating a third division championship, was ravaged by a fire which had started in the old wooden stand. 56 people died in the fire with many others scarred physically and mentally. The arrival of Geoffrey Richmond as chairman hailed a new horizon and City, under manager Paul Jewell, celebrated the millennium with promotion to the Premier ending a 77-year absence from the country's top division.

Halifax Town
Formed: 1911
Grounds: Sandhill Lane (1911), Exley (1919), The Shay (1921)
Football League: 1921-1993, 1997
Nicknames: Shaymen, Fax

Formed in a meeting at the Saddle Hotel, Halifax joined the Football League in 1921 as members of the

Third Division North. Like Odsal Stadium, the Shay was a former council rubbish tip and to make sure the players signed for Town, the manager used to meet prospective players at a nearby railway station and made sure they put pen to paper before they saw the state of the ground. When it looked like the club would fold in 1931, supporters rallied round to clear their debts. Halifax's great feats have been in FA Cup exploits – twice reaching the fifth round but never reaching any higher divisions in the league. Twice Halifax has suffered 13-0 defeats: at Stockport County in 1934 and Newport County in 1946. In the Stockport match, according to one contemporary, one of the Halifax players asked another what the score was and was told 'I don't know, but I think we're losing'. The term 'donkey', according to football writer David Pickering, used from the terraces throughout the country to illustrate a player's bad error, has associations at the Shay, for the 'Hee haw' chant that duplicates the slang term is said to have originated among Town fans during 1983-84.

Huddersfield Town
Formed: 1908
Grounds: Leeds Road and McAlpine Stadium (1994)
Football League: 1910
Nickname: The Terriers

The Leeds Road ground hosted football until the newly-built McAlpine Stadium replaced it in 1994. The ground had featured local matches since 1899 and when Town first moved there the facilities were so limited that the players used a nearby old tramcar as dressing rooms. Town's golden era was in the 1920s when Herbert Chapman, who had been at the ill-fated Leeds City, was their manager. Chapman eventually left for Arsenal as the team he helped build won the first division championship from 1924 to 1926 and finished second in 1923, 1927 and 1928, as well as winning the FA Cup in 1922. The club has gone from the top to the fourth division and back again and are currently in the first division (the old second division). After surviving a financial crisis after the Second World War (when it looked as though the club would close), a stand fire in 1950, and its floodlights felled by gales in the sixties, it made sense in the 90s to replace the old ailing ground along with the rundown Fartown home of the town's rugby team with one new modern stadium hosting both sports.

Hull City
Formed: 1904
Grounds: Boulevard (1904), Anlaby Road (1905), Boothferry Park (1946)
Football League: 1905
Nickname: The Tigers

Hull City is another club that has faced competition from its local rugby clubs, a position that was apparent when the club formed in 1904. Never a top flight club, one of Hull's most memorable seasons was their 1930 FA Cup run, which ended at the semi final. City have suffered a lot of uncertainty and at one time it looked as though Yorkshire might have the embarrassment of the club following Doncaster and Scarborough out of the league until they pulled around to avoid relegation. The Tigers have played at Boothferry Park since 1946 after moving from Anlaby Road. The club had bought the ground as early as 1930 and had a train station outside the ground where you could walk off the platform through the turnstile.

Leeds United

Formed: 1919
Ground: Elland Road
Football League: 1920
Nickname: The Peacocks

Elland Road, like many other leading West Riding grounds in the pioneer days of football, was a rugby ground which Holbeck Rugby Club used. The original Leeds team in the Football League was Leeds City who moved to Elland Road on their formation and acceptance into the league. Prior to the First World War, the legendary Herbert Chapman (later to have great success at Huddersfield Town and Arsenal) was manager, but when football returned after five years it was found the club were in trouble over illegal payments to players. A condition that saw Leeds City expelled from the league. United took their place in 1920 but it wasn't until the Don Revie era that the club achieved champion status. Leeds won the first division championship in 1969 and 1974, the FA Cup in 1972, the Fairs Cup in 1968 and 1971, and the League Cup in 1972. 1969 was their best season when they amassed a 34-game undefeated run.

The club dropped into the second division, returning to the first under Howard Wilkinson and culminating with the League Championship in 1993. Under manager David O'Leary they now have a side to rival that of the Revie era.

Middlesbrough

Formed: 1876
Grounds: Archery Ground, Albert Park (1876), Breckon Hill (1879), Linthorpe Round Ground (1882), Ayresome Park (1903), Riverside Stadium (1995)
Football League: 1899
Nicknames: Ironsides

Middlesbrough FC was formed during a discussion at a tripe supper in 1876. 'Borough turned professional in 1889 but reverted back to amateur status with great success in cup competition three years later, the club winning the amateur cup in 1895 and 1898. The club returned to professional football and re-joined the league in 1899. Famous for legendary goalscorers like George Camsell and Brian Clough, Middlesbrough has moved several times between the first and second divisions. Since moving to the Riverside Stadium in 1995 under Bryan Robson's management the club has already tasted promotion and relegation.

Rotherham United
Formed: 1925
Grounds: Red House (1878), Millmoor (1907)
Football League: 1925
Nickname: Merry Millers

After two earlier Rotherham teams (Rotherham Town 1893-96 and Rotherham County 1919-25) had graced the Football League, a merger between the two clubs saw Rotherham United join the league for the season 1925-26. The club had origins in a Thornhill United side that was founded in 1878 and later became Rotherham County. Town had joined the second division in 1893 but had dropped out after failing to win re-election in 1896. United have never made the league's top division but came within a whisker in the mid-fifties when they lost out on goal difference. A popular sports quiz question is who were the teams to contest the first ever League Cup final in 1961. Rotherham, in probably their greatest moment, were beaten by Aston Villa. In between the wars, Rotherham once got lost in fog and didn't turn up for a fixture at Hartlepool.

Sheffield United

Formed: 1889
Ground: Bramall Lane
Football League: 1892
Nickname: The Blades

Founded by an offshoot of the County Cricket Club in 1889, the club were originally referred to as the 'Cutlers'. Difficulty in fielding a team led to player recruitment in Scotland. By 1892 the team had progressed enough to join the league. Sheffield United hit a golden patch and before 1925 the club had won the FA Cup four times, with their only first division title coming in 1898. United are fierce rivals of Wednesday and the pendulum between the two has swung backwards and forwards as each club has taken its turn as the city's leading team. Derby days in recent seasons have been sparse and Wednesday fans have missed their match-day custom of not eating bacon because United play in red and white. Embarrassed into playing fourth division football, United won that league in 1982 arriving in the Premier division in its initial season before dropping back into the first division. United were the first team to score ten goals in a match, but did it have something to do with the Port Vale goalkeeper losing his spectacles in the mud?

Sheffield Wednesday

Formed: 1867
Grounds: Dronfield (1867), Olive Grove (1887), Owlerton (now Hillsborough 1899)
Football League: 1892
Nickname: Formerly Blades now Owls which originates from Owlerton.

The Sheffield Association is one of the oldest of its

kind in England. Formed in 1857, Sheffield FC (North East Counties League) is the oldest football club in the world and Hallam, from the same league, boasts the oldest football ground in the world. The original fixture between the two sides is another first.

Wednesday is the oldest surviving league club. Again there is a cricket connection for the club is a descendant of the Sheffield Wednesday Cricket Club (the name derives from the players' half-holiday meeting day). The club moved to Owlerton in 1899, the ground later being renamed Hillsborough, a name that will be forever associated with the disaster that took place there. Wednesday's glory days were pre-1930 when they recorded four league championships (more than any other Yorkshire club) and an FA Cup win in 1896.

York City

Formed: 1922
Grounds: Fulford Gate (1922), Bootham Crescent (1932)
Football League: 1929
Nicknames: the Minster men

There have been earlier York City teams in the town, but the present side were formed in 1922. They gained admission to the Third Division North in 1929 and never left the division until it joined with the Third Division South to form a third and fourth division at the back end of the fifties. Leaving Fulford Gate, City moved to their present ground, Bootham Crescent, which they had purchased from York Cricket Club in 1932. The club had a brief period in the second division in the seventies and although York have enjoyed a series of giant-killing cup wins against Premier sides recently, one of their best remembered exploits was in the FA Cup in

1955. Led by the goalscoring feats of Alf Bottom, York almost made it to Wembley. The great Newcastle team of the time knocked them out in the semi-final and United were that impressed with Bottom (the rib of a lot of jokes at the time) they signed him. Sadly Bootham, which could once hold 28,000, is now limited to a quarter of that size.

FORMER LEAGUE CLUBS

Doncaster Rovers
Formed: 1879
Ground: Belle Vue (1922)
Football League: 1901-03, 1904-05, 1923-1998
Nickname: The Dons

Formed in 1879, Doncaster turned professional in 1885 and entered Football League service in 1901 as a member of the second division. They lost their league status in 1903, but returned the following year only to drop out again in 1905. Rovers came back for a third spell in 1923, the return co-inciding with the club taking residence at Belle Vue. The town's supporters helped build most of the ground and such was the condition of the grass at Belle Vue that Wembley offered £10,000 for it in 1970. For a while the ground had a pigeon box high in the stand where an owl nested and the story was if the owl came out during the game Rovers were certain to win. Before their demise from the Football League in 1998, the club hit a catalogue of problems, not least of all a dilapidated Belle Vue. For a club that once had all its players put on the transfer list by the then manager Dave Mackay their relegation to the Conference has since seen a fresh wind blow through Belle Vue – don't be surprised to see the return of the club to its rightful home.

Scarborough
Formed: 1879
Grounds: North Marine Cricket Ground (1879) Recreation Ground (1887) Athletic Ground (later called McCain 1888)
Football League: 1987-99
Nickname: Sea dogs or Borough

Like several Yorkshire clubs Scarborough have their origins in a cricket club and first played at the ground on North Marine Road. Through time in the Yorkshire League and later the Alliance (now Conference) Scarborough got their green light for league football in 1987 when they became the first team to gain promotion from the Conference to the fourth division. The stadium name was switched to McCain after the oven chip king. Despite several innovations like forming a crèche for supporters and forming a Rugby League team, Scarborough has struggled to get the locals interested. The team lost their status in the last minute of the last match of the season in 1999: when they thought they had survived, a late goal in another game scored by an out playing goalkeeper sent them down.

Bradford Park Avenue
Formed: 1907
Ground: Park Avenue (1907-73), Valley Parade (1973-74) (since reformation as a Saturday club in 1988) Manningham Mills, Bramley RL, Batley RL and presently Horsfall Stadium, Bradford.
Football League: 1908-70.
Nickname: The Avenue

Like Valley Parade, Park Avenue was first a rugby ground. Avenue formed in 1907 and had a season in the Southern League before joining the Football League second division in the 1908-09 season. Reaching the first division at the outbreak of the war, Avenue suffered successive relegations at the start of the 20s to the Third Division North. Before the decade was out, the team returned to the second division. The club enjoyed a good side in the late forties, but by the time the sixties arrived were in the fourth division. Promotion into division three only lasted two seasons. Forced to sell leading scorer Kevin Hector the club went further into decline and lost its league status in 1970, surviving in the Northern Premier until 1974. Kept alive by a bunch of die-hards in Bradford Sunday football, the club was reformed after interest was revived by a book on the old team, and since the reformation in 1988, Avenue have got back to Northern Premier football. A question often posed is would things have been any different if the club had appointed legend, Bill Shankley, as manager when he was one of two applicants for the job in 1953?

Middlesbrough Ironopolis
Ground: Paradise Ground
Football League: 1893-94

Middlesbrough Ironopolis, now long forgotten, had one season in the Football League. Looking set to eclipse amateur rivals Middlesbrough as the town's top club and despite a quarterfinal FA Cup appearance around the time, the club lasted one season in the league.

YORKSHIRE	FA Cup winners	First Division League Champions
Sheffield Wednesday	1896	
Sheffield United		1898
Sheffield United	1899	
Sheffield United	1902	
Sheffield Wednesday		1903
Sheffield Wednesday		1904
Sheffield Wednesday	1907	
Bradford City	1911	
Barnsley	1912	
Sheffield United	1915	
Huddersfield Town	1922	
Huddersfield Town		1924
Sheffield United	1925	
Huddersfield Town		1925
Huddersfield Town		1926
Sheffield Wednesday		1929
Sheffield Wednesday		1930
Sheffield Wednesday	1935	
Leeds United		1969
Leeds United	1972	
Leeds United		1974
Leeds United		1992

'Shack'

Who was Yorkshire's greatest footballer? A name on a lot of the older generation's tongues would be the colourful and charismatic Len Shackleton. It is a certainty that if Shack, with his individual skill and creative talent, was gracing today's game when players are on a level with pop stars, he would be treated as a God by the media. Because he is often portrayed as a football rebel it is a shame that in time he will probably be more well known for an empty page in his autobiography *The Crown Prince of Soccer* (Len left a blank page in his book with the heading 'The Average Directors Knowledge of Football') and for some of his quotes in later life as a journalist (writing about the time when his old club Newcastle were going through a re-building period Shack related 'I've heard of people selling dummies not buying them!') than for his feats on the field – like his comeback game for England in 1954 when he capped an out-standing return by chipping the keeper for a fine individual goal.

Born in Bradford in 1922 and educated at Carlton High (burnt down in 1949), Shackleton graduated to the England schoolboys team at the age of fourteen. On leaving school he went to Arsenal but his frailty and size went against him. He returned home and in 1940 joined the second division Bradford Park Avenue. His amazing dribbling skill and rocket shot 'The Shack Special' saw him achieve rave notices and before the war was out Newcastle had paid £13000 for him. Has anyone made a more striking debut? Shack was a sensation. He smacked in six in a 13-1 riot against Newport County. Halfway through 1947-48 the unheard of happened: Newcastle sold him to the 'enemy' Sunderland. This was nearly as bad as switching sides to the Germans during the war in some supporters' eyes. The fee was £25,050

– fifty pounds more than the record Notts. County had paid for Tommy Lawton.

Len played in the victory international at Hampden against Scotland after the war after which his England appearances were spasmodic, but in 1954, at the age of 32, he was brought back and put the icing on the cake with his first England goal. In nine seasons he made six appearances – farcical figures when one considers the depth of his talent. Shack served Sunderland until 1958 (320 games, 97 goals). The season after he finished, the club was relegated to the second division for the first time. Following his retirement Shack worked consistently for the popular press and it is comforting to note that despite his record of only half a dozen caps, several publications have included him in compilations of 'soccer greats' and that many of the things that grieved him in his so-called 'anarchist days' have come to pass.

HORSE RACING

Dating back to Roman times, horse racing is one of Yorkshire's oldest sports. With nine picturesque, characteristic and individual courses featuring both flat and National Hunt racing and including the jewels of Doncaster and York where some of the country's top races are held, a 'day at the races' is a well-established Yorkshire tradition. The country's first race course was reputed to be at Wetherby near Kirkby Overblow, whilst one record Yorkshire can be proud of is that the oldest steeplechase, the famous Kiplingcotes Derby first run in 1619, still takes place in the East Riding.

Beverley
Course Flat
Racing on the Westwood, an area of common land just outside the East Riding cathedral city, dates back to 1690 and the land is the site of today's course. Beverley had its own star in *Rapid Lad* – the safe bet won 12 races at the course between 1983 and 1989 and as a result Beverley now stages the Rapid Lad Handicap in his honour.

Catterick
Course Flat and National Hunt
Well supported by trainers from Middleham, the major training area of the North, Catterick has race origins

which stretch back into the seventeenth century, with riding on the present course since 1793. Facilities were improved considerably when a new grandstand opened in 1998. *God's Solution* became a Catterick institution when it won the same handicap in successive times from 1985 to 1989. In 1990, the race was named God's Solution Handicap to respect the horse's feat. The old stager couldn't produce the finish and came in third but, not to be outdone, God must have been looking over its shoulder the following year for the horse returned as a ten year old, won the race for a sixth time and promptly retired.

Doncaster
Course Flat and National Hunt
Home to Britain's fifth and oldest classic, the St Leger, and the Lincoln Handicap (Lincoln closed in 1964) which heralds the opening of the flat season. The Leger was first run in 1776 and today is classed as the Northern Derby Day. In Doncaster races featured on the Town Moor where the present course lies, although the first two Legers were run at nearby Cantley Common. Acknowledged as having one of the best surfaces in the country, Doncaster has been the venue for several celebrated St Leger winners. In 1985 *Oh So Sharp* achieved everlasting fame by winning the 1000 Guineas and The Oaks in the same year and, in 1987, *Reference Point* did the famous double of Derby and Leger wins. In 1995 the charismatic Italian Frankie Dettori rode *Classic Cliché* to the 1000th victory of his career. The other two main races at Donny are the Racing Post Trophy (started in 1961) and the Doncaster Trophy, which goes back to the earliest racing days in the area.

Pontefract

Course Flat

A favourite course for miners and popular as a night time venue, Pontefract dates back to the seventeenth century. The longest flat racing circuit in the county, the course was horseshoe-shaped until the ends were joined up in 1983. It was kept open during the war when both the Lincoln and Manchester handicaps were run there.

Redcar

Course Flat

The course became prominent through its owner Lord Zetland who installed the popular Zetland Old Cup and the Two Year Old Trophy. Before the course was opened in 1871, racing had taken place on nearby sands. Princess Anne won her first flat race at Redcar.

Ripon

Course Flat

Ripon was an area with several courses. Racing commenced in the seventeenth century with the present site seeing its first races in 1900. Ripon's main race is the six-furlong Great St Wilfred Handicap.

Thirsk

Course Flat

Meetings have been held at Thirsk since 1855. Like 'Ponty' it was open over the war period during which it held the 1940 Leger, which was re-named The Yorkshire Leger for the occasion. Mark Birch has been a popular rider at Thirsk in recent years. The most noted race held here is the Hunt Cup.

Wetherby

Course National Hunt

Wetherby's original racing track was on the Wharfe banks around 1840. The present course, which has been updated with a new stand, opened in 1891. Yorkshire's sole jump course, Wetherby's best known chases are the Charlie Hall Memorial Chase (3 miles), Rowland Mayrick Handicap (3 mile, 1 furlong) and Castleford Chase (2 mile).

York

Course Flat

Yorkshire's finest and, boasting a recent new grand-stand, recognised as the best racecourse in the North. Immensely popular, as indeed York is itself, racing has gone on in York since the Romans ruled. An afternoon's racing often followed the hanging of the area's robbers. The first official race in Knavesmire followed a display of public executions and when poor Dick Turpin, a noted horseman himself, got his neck pulled in 1739, a cele-bration of races followed. In 1851 100,000 fans struggled for space to watch a race between two classic winners *Flying Dutchman* and *Voltiguers* which the for-mer won. The three group one races in York are the International Stakes (commenced 1972 and links with earlier Eclipse and Champion stakes), the Yorkshire Oaks (run on the same day as famous Ebor Handicap) and the Nunthorpe Stakes. The first time the International Stakes was run it saw that great horse *Brigadier Gerard* record its only defeat out of 18.

'Smoking Joe Mercer' – a nickname contrived because of the habitual pipe in his mouth ...

Joe Mercer

Often confused with the great footballer and manager of the same name, Joe Mercer, who was born in Bradford, had 35 years as one of the country's leading jockeys. When Joe finally hung up his saddle in 1985 he had amassed 2810 winners and at the time was fourth in the all-time winners list behind three other legends: Sir Gordon Richards, Lester Piggott and Doug Smith. 'Smoking Joe Mercer', a nickname contrived because of the habitual pipe in his mouth, will always be associated with that great runner *Brigadier Gerard* which he rode in many of his triumphs, including the 1971 2000 guineas. Often referred to as the greatest jockey never to win the Derby, Joe was expert at pulling races out of the fire. He also was not one for over use of the whip.

Racing was in the Mercer blood. Joe's family left the smoky mill city of Bradford when Joe was nine after his father, Emmanuel, who had been a coach painter, found alternative work. He was a big racing fan as were his four sons who each tried their hand at being a jockey. Elder brother Manny who had toughened himself up in the long hours of the Bradford mills became the first apprentice. Joe followed Manny into an apprenticeship at a stable at 12 and like his brother became a boy wonder.

Joe went on to win eight classic races, emulating Manny by winning the 1000 and 2000 guineas, but perhaps Joe's greatest performance was coming to terms with his brother's death on the course in 1959 when he died from a fall. Winning his first classic at 18 in 1953 and others in the next three decades, Joe climaxed his career by becoming champion jockey at 45.

Joe Mercer's classic wins

1000 Guineas 1974 *Highclere*,1979 *Once in a Million*

Oaks 1953 *Ambiguity*

2000 Guineas 1971 *Brigadier Gerard*

St Leger 1965 *Provoke*, 1974 *Bustino*, 1980 *Light Cavalry*, 1981 *Cut Above*

GREYHOUNDS

Though not enjoying the popularity it once had as a spectator sport, greyhound racing is still strong particularly in South Yorkshire where the sport was always linked with the mining fraternity. The sport's cloth cap and meat pie image no longer exists as tracks advertise greyhounds as part of a package night out incorporating a meal. There is no need to leave the warmth of the bar to place a bet and arrays of TV sets show all the races live.

Introduced into this country from America in 1926 dog tracks spread all over the country with enough interest for several meetings a week. Belle Vue (Manchester), in which locality racing is still popular, was the first greyhound stadium to open in the country, quickly followed in 1927 by Greenfield Stadium at Dudley Hill in Bradford which had an earlier history as an athletics ground. Interest was enough for a second stadium, the City dog track at Legrams Lane, in the early thirties.

The sport, with betting its main attraction, has had more than a passing interest from one or two of life's shady characters. In 1937 revelations came out that a kennel boy at Greenfield had been feeding some of the dogs with what the youngster genuinely believed to be mints. In fact the 'mints' turned out to be sleeping tablets (provided by a bookmaker) which explained the dogs' lack of interest in chasing the hare.

Greenfield, which had a brief flirtation with speedway

when racing stopped at Odsal for a while, closed in 1969 after 4,790 meetings. One of the few tracks with undersoil heating, the last-ever winner was *Tanroyd Jack*. The City dog track had closed a few years earlier never recovering from a fire. 77 year old scrap dealer Luke Delaney who bought all the tracks timber, had helped build the stadium 33 years earlier.

Keighley's track at Parkwood Stadium ran from 1947 to 1975 when the planned Aire Valley Road put an end to meetings which had dwindled to 400 from 1500 in its heyday. Parkwood was the scene of one of greyhound's most intriguing stories. The year was 1965 and Parkwood was holding a meeting on the May bank holiday. A few months earlier in January, Britain's wonder dog and favourite for the year's greyhound derby, *Hi Joe*, had been kidnapped from its home in London. An Irishman from Bedfordshire rang Keighley to inquire about entering a dog at the bank holiday meeting and on

... had it been raining, it's a good bet that the black dye would have run to reveal a brown Hi Joe underneath ...

the day of the racing, four Irish lads turned up with a black greyhound in the back of a car. The dog ran in a 308-yard race and after being crowded out at the first bend showed an amazing burst of speed to finish second.

It was a surprise when the dog's handlers wanted the dog, which was named Rusty because it had bits of brown showing, to run in the next 508-yard race because dogs normally needed a couple of days rest after a race. The organisers were a dog short and agreed and the meeting's backers, recognising a good thing, saw the dog heavily backed at 2-1. The dog sailed home winning by a cricket pitch length smashing the track record in a time of 29.05 seconds. Every spectator realised that the dog was no ordinary greyhound. The handlers stole away quickly returning later for their £100 winnings.

The matter was reported to the police. Had it been raining, it's a good bet that the black dye would have run to reveal a brown *Hi Joe* underneath. The following February after a phone call the dog was found safe and unharmed in Dunstable. *Santa Pet* won the last ever race at Parkwood and with Elland Road now no longer catering for racing there was talk of reviving the sport in Bradford in 1994. Unfortunately the proportions of Valley Parade, the proposed venue, were unsuitable.

SPEEDWAY

Boomerangs

Since the first speedway meeting in this country, held in Epping Forest in 1928, speedway has had more revivals than *My Fair Lady* and *Doctor Dolittle* put together. Originally split into north and south team league divisions in which Leeds was a member of the north section from 1930-31 and Sheffield the only Yorkshire member of the First National League in 1932, the sport had its real boom years after the war.

Showman and entrepreneur Johnnie Hoskins, that great pioneer of speedway from down under, decided that the Odsal Bowl in Bradford would be an ideal venue to promote his sport and after 20,000 turned up for the first open meeting, Hoskins who had been a war time RAF instructor, entered his Odsal Boomerangs in the 1946 National League. The other five teams were West Ham, Wimbledon, Wembley and New Cross all of London; and Belle Vue of Manchester – the only other Northern team.

After a lengthy period of war, sport was booming in England and crowds very rarely dipped below 20,000. Riders were quickly adopted as heroes. These were the days when few had cars; motor bikes were an easier option and progression from bike to car seemed to be the norm. Unfortunately too many youngsters tried to emulate their heroes on the way home from the meeting.

This author well remembers another facet of Odsal at

the time. Bradford Northern rugby team played in the stadium in the afternoon and not long after the final whistle crowds were already forming for the Saturday night's speedway. The game was to hide in the ground either in toilets or in bushes on the top side. We were always found out and with mams not able to pay for two events the other option was to wait until the speedway started and then take it in turn to plead with the turnstile operators 'Let me in mister'. This sometimes worked and we were able to jump over the turnstile.

Speedway was a very dangerous sport and in June 1946 Odsal was the scene of a track death. 'Aussie' Rosenfield, a Huddersfield rider who had been trying to get into speedway for years, hit the wheels of another bike and was thrown head first into the fencing. Fracturing his skull he was dead in a fortnight. When another rider, Colin Wilson, fractured his skull and never rode again Odsal was issued with an ultimatum: 'alter the track or lose your permit'. Bruce Booth, quarry owner and government stores contractor, took a gang of his men and the track became more oval and was reduced in length from 382 yards to 370.

Australian Max Grosskreutz was Odsal's best rider of the late forties. In 1949 he declined to return from Australia to ride for Odsal, but then at the last minute flew to England. Unfortunately for Max he broke a pelvis at Belle Vue and never rode again. Bruce Booth had replaced Hoskins as promoter with Eric Langton who had been the first rider to try Odsal in 1945, team manager. The big story of 1949 was the unheard of £3000 that Belle Vue were willing to pay for Odsal rider Oliver Hart whose leg-trailing style of riding had made him a speedway legend. A second tragedy occurred in July 1949 when Joe Abbott, who had earlier survived a fractured spine, was killed in a pit-bend crash. Amazingly on the same day that 48-year-old Abbott died, Jack Sheard, who had been in speedway since 1928, was killed riding for Halifax at Norwich in a second division fixture. Both riders lived in Burnley and were born in the same street.

Tudors and the Black Prince
In 1950 Odsal changed the name from Boomerangs to Tudors. Mirfield rider Eddie Rigg matured to one of the best riders in England and carried the Tudors on his shoulders. Rigg rode for England and finished seventh in the world final at Wembley where second-half engine failure curtailed his chance of winning. Halifax had commenced second division riding at the Shay in the late forties (Booth's wife Norma had been team manager), but dwindling crowds and tax-rate difficulties saw the

club close down and most of the team move to Odsal.

By far the best capture was Arthur Forrest whose immaculate shiny leathers and upright style saw him labelled the Black Prince. A nursery rider at Odsal when sixteen, Arthur quickly became one of the country's top track men on his return.

Forrest had another Arthur for a rival at Odsal: Arthur Wright whose parents had owned the garage on Odsal Top roundabout. Though they didn't ride together, both riders having different team partners, the two Arthur's were untouchable at Odsal. Wright once recording an 18-point maximum in a test match against Australia on the track. The Prince won the British match race championship (golden helmet) in 1954 and defended it successfully against the likes of Ronnie Moore and Brian Crutcher. Forrest's best attempt in the Wembley world final came in 1956 when he finished third behind Ove Fundin and Ronnie Moore. Arthur was in it until he veered in the last race. He won the run off for third place with the pint-sized 1955 winner Peter Craven. Odsal folded the following year and when speedway recommenced in Bradford it was in the Provincial League at Greenfield.

Dukes and an Odsal World Champion
Odsal youngster Nigel Boocock who was a reserve at Wembley in 1956 moved to Coventry and became one of England's top riders of the next decade (fourth in world final in 1969). And it was Nigel's younger brother Eric (best in world final 6th) who became the kingpin at the Shay when speedway was revived in Halifax in the sixties. The Halifax Dukes moved over to Odsal when the stadium was revamped to hold the world final. The move to the new-look Odsal was tinged with tragedy when the

Dukes leading rider, Kenny Carter (Kenny had won the world pairs in 1983 with Peter Collins and was tipped as a future world champion), died in upsetting circumstances.

With the Ham brothers Alan and Bobby (well known in Bradford football circles) at the helm, Bradford speedway went through its most successful spell. However, despite the Hams bringing in the country's top riders like Joe Screen and Mark Loram interest never rose much above 2000.

In 1992 Odsal had its world champion when 26-year-old Eaglescliffe-born and rave music-fan Gary Havelock, whose career had started with Middlesbrough, fulfilled early promise and took the world title.

Uncertainty about Odsal stadium's proposed development and whether it would include a speedway track saw Odsal fold. Hull and Sheffield have since carried the Yorkshire flag but since the introduction of a speedway Grand Prix and TV interest, speedway looks to be going through yet another revival.

GOLF

Once considered the sport of the businessman and the affluent, golf is now accessible to most people and, as recent crowds have proved at big events in the country, an ever-increasing spectator sport. The Yorkshire Union of Golf Clubs boasts records dating back to 1894 and there are around 160 courses in the region.

Yorkshire's foremost clubs are: **Moortown** (Alwoodly) which was the original home of the Ryder Cup and where Peter Allis, now the voice of golf, was the club's professional; **Fulford** (York) a venue of several big golf tournaments; **Pannal** (Harrogate); and **Ganton** (a few miles from Scarborough in the tranquil Vale of Pickering) which gained a place in a recent publication of the world's top 100 golf courses.

Harry Vardon who hailed from the Channel Islands and was *the* golfer at the turn of the century with six open championships (1896, 1898, 1899, 1901, 1903 and 1911 and second place in 1900, 1901 and 1912) had strong Yorkshire connections. Born in 1870 Vardon became a greenkeeper at Studley Royal, Ripon in 1890. By the time he won the first of his opens he was the resident pro at Ganton. An all-round sportsman Harry played a good standard of cricket and once broke his arm playing football for Ganton. After his fifth open win Vardon developed tuberculosis but returned in triumph after an eight-year gap to win the 1911 title.

The only Yorkshire golfer to win a place in the all-time top 100 golfers was Leeds born **Howard Clark** of whom it's often been said that if his temperament had matched his talent he would have been an open or big classic winner. Howard won eleven European victories, a 1984 PGA championship at Wentworth and made six Ryder Cup appearances.

One of the country's top players of recent years also had a Yorkshire background. Born in Scotland, **Colin Montgomerie** spent part of his childhood in Ilkley and went to school at Ghyll Royd in Burley from 1972 to 1974. Already playing golf most nights after school in Burley, Monty's golf graduation was carried on at the Ilkley club.

CYCLING

Cycling is not as popular as it used to be – our overfull polluted highways and strangulated country roads on summer weekends have helped prevent that – but Yorkshire's open spaces and beautiful scenery still provide a haven for cyclists from all over the country.

The first cyclists touring club was formed in Harrogate in 1878 and by 1882 there were 528 known cycling clubs in Britain. The big cycling boom started just before 1900 and, with long-distance riding both in races and against the clock in vogue, the world's greatest touring race, The Tour de France, commenced in 1903. Easy access from the country's big cities to quicker country lanes has seen Yorkshire produce its own share of cycle champions over the years.

Brian Robinson of Mirfield along with Tony Hoar became the first British rider to finish the Tour de France in 1955. Brian then achieved another first for Yorkshire when he was the first Englishman to win a tour stage, a feat he repeated again in 1960.

Tony Simpson was another rider with connections in the county. Tony was the first British rider to wear the race leader's yellow jersey in 1962. In 1965 he showed exceptional courage when he fell on the tour and it was touch and go whether doctors amputated his arm; then in the same season he won the Tour of Lombardy and

World Road Race Championship. The latter is another first for Britain. Two years later Simpson died after collapsing during the tour race whilst climbing Mount Ventoux.

Arthur Metcalfe: In 1966 the Leeds rider had an amazing year winning the British all rounder championship against the clock over 50 and 100 miles, the National Amateur Road race and the 12-hour distance race. Earlier he had won the 1964 Milk Race and competed in the Tour de France.

Dave Baker: Dronfield's Dave Baker rates as Britain's most successful mountain bike racer. Winning national points series in 1993 and 1994 and the national championship three times from 1992 to 1994, Baker made his mark on the world stage when he was third in the UCI World Championship and won a round of the Cup series in 1993.

Beryl Burton: Yorkshire's most popular cyclist was 'our Beryl' who so dominated the sport that the Morley lass who could take on and beat men is overwhelmingly revered – and until recently probably the only woman cyclist 99 per cent of the population has heard of. Known chiefly as a time trialist, Beryl won an unprecedented list of British titles and few women could beat her at any distance. She was all round champion 25 times from 1959 to 1983 (from the ages of 18 to 46) and won 72 individual time trial races, 12 road race titles and 14 track pursuit titles. In 1967 in a 12 hour time trial Beryl covered 446.19km which was then 9.25 beyond the men's record. In the following year she rode 100 miles in 3 hours 55 minutes 5 seconds, 12 years after the first

Englishman had broke 4 hours for the distance. In world championships at individual pursuit, Beryl's impressive record runs to five gold, three silver and three bronze medals, whilst at road racing, to prove she wasn't just a clock rider, she won two gold and a silver. Honoured by becoming the first woman to be allowed to compete at the highest level with men in the Grand Prix de Nations, she was awarded the MBE in 1964 and the OBE in 1968. She held over 50 time trial records including world records at 3k and 20k. One of Beryl's proudest moments came in 1972 when her daughter Denise joined her as a member of the British team, the first mother and daughter combination to do so.

Yvonne McGregor: the first British woman ever to win an Olympic cycling medal: At 39 years the oldest-ever female cycling medallist, Bradford's Yvonne McGregor took the bronze medal in the 3,000 metres individual pursuit at the 2000 Olympics in Sydney. The medal crowned a remarkable eight-year career in which she won Commonwealth gold and bronze, a World Championship bronze and came fourth in the Atlanta Olympic Games.

RUGBY LEAGUE

Often and rightfully labelled the toughest team sport in the world, Rugby League has witnessed several attempts in recent years to broaden its boundaries and interest. However,the sport still has, and probably *will* only have, a Yorkshire and Lancashire domain. Yet the advent of Super League with its razzmatazz and American-style tag names *has* taken the game up a gear and introduced it to a younger family-orientated audience – a far cry from its earlier cloth cap image. Though there are always casualties in 'progress', it is sad to see some of the established names from the game's history playing no part in the elite league.

RUGBY LEAGUE RECORD SCORERS

The record for tries in a season has stood since 1913-14 when Huddersfield flyer **Albert Rosenfield** topped his own earlier record of 78 by crossing the line 80 times and it is doubtful if the Rosenfield landmark will ever be beaten. The nearest since has been the bald, bandy-legged, Australian try machine **Brian Bevan** who reached 72 for Warrington in the fifties. Bevan, the most unlikely looking rugby player, holds the career record of tries – 796 from 1945 to his last game in 1964. The best in modern times has come from **Ellery Hanley** from the invincible Wigan team of the eighties. Hanley scored 63 times in 1986-87, the joint eighth best ever. The highest number of tries in a game is eleven by **George West** of Hull Kingston Rovers in 1905. This has been threatened a couple of times in recent seasons by modern greats **Martin Offiah** and **Shaun Edwards** who both scored ten. Offiah has made great inroads into the all-time try scoring record list in the last decade and has achieved the feat of being leading scorer for the season six times – another record.

The immortal **Jim Sullivan**, one of the game's biggest legends, was the greatest goal kicker Rugby League has seen. In the eighteen seasons from 1921 to 1939 he topped the leading goalscorer's list sixteen times – 194 being his best. He created another record with 22 goals in one match in 1925 and with the demands of the modern game Sullivan's appearance record, which stands at 928, will never be beaten.

Another bandy-legged 'baldie', Welshman **Lewis Jones**, equalled Sullivan's season record in 1956-57, only for Oldham full back, **Bernard Ganley**, to top the 200 mark with 221 the season after. It was another Welsh rugby union convert, **Dave Watkins**, who became the next and present holder with 221 for Salford in 1972-73. The phenomenal scoring three-quarter **Neil Fox,** who played the majority of his football with Wakefield Trinity, overtook Sullivan's points aggregate of 6022 and finished his career at forty with 6220 points.

Ben Gronow of Huddersfield became the first player to reach 300 points in a season (332 in 1919-20). Sullivan took his record in 1922 when he scored 349 and then hit an incredible 406 points in 1933-34. **Lewis Jones**

made a mockery of Sullivan's feat when he gathered 496 in 1956-57. Fox twice reached the 450 mark with Watkins coming the nearest to Jones's feat by scoring 473 in 1971-72 and finishing an agonising three points short the season after with 493. With the advent of four points for a try instead of three surprisingly the record stays intact. **John Wasyliw** reached 490 in 1992-93 with the Keighley Cougars.

The introduction of the four points try has seen several sides top the century in a game. The biggest win is now Huddersfield's 142-4, 1994 Regal trophy victory over Blackpool Gladiators, with Barrow's 138-0 win over Nottingham City, (who became the third team ever in 1991-92 not to win a game in a season), sharing the points record difference in the same season.

YORKSHIRE RUGBY LEAGUE GREATS
Mick Sullivan – Great Britain's Record Scoring Winger
Born in 1934, Sullivan was a product of the famous Shaw Cross Boys Club. Joining Huddersfield he rose from obscurity to play in the World Cup in 1954 when Britain were the first-ever winners under Sullivan's Fartown captain Dave Valentine – one of the first Scots to make it in Rugby League.

Moving to Wigan in 1957 for a Rugby League record of £9,500, Mick played in winning-Wembley sides in 1957 and 1959 before moving to Wigan's rivals St Helens for £11000, appearing in a third winning Wembley team, against Wigan. With a reputation for being awkward, Sullivan played his rugby hard and par-ticularly liked stirring up the Australians. On tour in 1958 Sullivan scored a hat trick in a 40-17 thrashing of

When bottles and oranges were thrown onto the field Sullivan angered them more by eating an orange and washing it down with a drink from one of the bottles.

the Aussies in Sydney and shattered the tour record of 38 tries. It was on this tour that a Sullivan try (which had come after Mick finished off a length of the field movement) upset the Aussies. When bottles and oranges were thrown onto the field Sullivan angered them more by eating an orange and washing it down with a drink from one of the bottles. At the end of his career Mick returned to Yorkshire playing for York and Dewsbury and had a short spell in coaching.

In his career from 1952 to 1966 the winger scored 342 tries. In 51 international appearances he scored 45 tries, at the time 15 more than second placed Billy Boston.

The Foxs of Sharlston

From the Yorkshire mining village of Sharlston near Pontefract came three rugby playing brothers who all achieved fame, some of it notoriously, in the world of Rugby League. Older brothers Peter and Don Fox both played at local club Featherstone whilst Neil signed for Featherstone's traditional rivals Wakefield Trinity who were *the* team of the early 1960s.

Don, first in a fine tradition of Featherstone scrumhalves (Marchant, Dooler, Nash and Deryck Fox were to follow), later moved into the pack when he became heavier. Don joined his brother at Wakefield and achieved his minute of lasting fame in the famous 1968 watersplash final between Wakefield and Leeds – a freak monsoon before the game made conditions farcical and when it looked like Leeds had won the game with a late try, Wakefield scored in the last minute. All was needed to win the game was a conversion in front of the posts. Neil, who was Trinity's usual kicker, was absent from the game through injury and Don missed the last kick of the game to give Leeds the cup 11-10. Replayed film of the kick with Eddie Waring's commentary has been featured regularly on TV and the incident is certainly one of the most dramatic moments in sport. Emulating his brother who had won the Lance Todd Trophy in 1962 was scant consolation. (The Foxs' feat of brothers winning the Lance Todd has been equalled by the Paul brothers Robbie (in 1997) and Henry (in 2000).

Neil started his league career as a strapping, 16-year-old full back/centre at Trinity in 1956. He played his last game in the opening match of the 1979-80 season for Bradford Northern, joining the elite who have played in a game at the age of 40. A great goal kicker Neil was a powerful centre, deadly near the line, with one of the most feared hand offs in Rugby League. Like Don, when he lost mobility he became a pack leader. The phenomenal points scorer passed the legendary Jim Sullivan, and his 6220 points will take some beating. Neil amassed 2575 goals (1836 for Wakefield Trinity in 19 sessions) and scored 358 tries (he also holds the Trinity try record with 272). Only Sullivan scored more points (2867) and Sullivan and Gus Risman played more games. Fox retired after 828 games, of which 28 were substitute appearances which included games for Bradford Northern in two spells, York, Bramley, Hull Kingston Rovers and Huddersfield as well as Wakefield.

Never achieving the heights of his brothers as a player, Peter played at Batley and Hull Kingston Rovers before trying his hand at coaching. He guided Featherstone to cup glory, Bramley to promotion and took Bradford to a championship double. He later had a short spell as Great Britain Coach (Don played once and Neil thirty times amassing 237 points for his country) and won acclaim when his 'dads army' team beat the Aussies.

Roger the Dodger
Born in Castleford in 1947 Roger Millward achieved his early fame as a star of televised junior rugby. Naturally the diminutive scrum half signed for Castleford but unfortunately at the time the club had the best pair of half backs in the league in Alan Hardisty and Keith

Hepworth (the pair had played together since they were seven years old and the only other pair to share equal understanding were Stan Kielty and Ken Dean of earlier Halifax fame). Roger was an obvious target for other clubs and after Bradford Northern had hiccuped at the £6000 fee, Hull Kingston Rovers bought him and what a bargain he became making 401 appearances for Rovers – his record of 207 tries for the club still stands today. An international at 18, and only 5ft 4in tall, the half back was at his elusive best in 1967-68 when he finished league leading scorer with 38 tries. His ability to make the gap and then produce the speed to take advantage saw Millward make 29 appearances for Britain and 17 for England with only the Sullivans, Jim and Mick, above him. Millward played at a time when we could beat Australia and one of his best remembered games came in Sydney in 1970 when he scored 20 points (7 goals, 2 tries) in a 28-7 win. He climaxed his career when he led Rovers in the all-Hull 1980 Rugby League Cup final. A series of broken jaws finished his career and he left the game after an unsuccessful attempt at coaching.

Ellery Hanley

To many eyes Ellery Hanley has been the nearest thing to perfection in the modern game. Single mindedness, great presence, dedication, a great game reader and thinker, versatility (he played for his country on the wing, centre stand off and full back), strength of pace and elusiveness are all Ellery Hanley attributes.

His try-scoring feat at Bradford Northern soon brought him to the attention of the rest of the Rugby League world. His 55 in 1984-85 was the first time a player had scored over fifty since 1961-62. A fall out at Northern saw Wigan move in for him and he was the icing on the cake for a Wigan side which dominated the eighties. A later move to loose forward gave him another dimension and after winning every honour with Wigan several times, he moved to his hometown Leeds for another big money deal. There was criticism over the fee Leeds payed for a player of Hanley's age but Ellery proved he wasn't a spent force. After his retirement in 1995 Ellery had amassed 428 tries, only Martin Offiah being above him from the modern game. His first game as coach was in charge of Great Britain and his side beat Australia at Wembley. There was a controversial spell in charge at St Helens before he left to take an engagement in Rugby Union.

ODSAL STADIUM

It is not long back that Odsal Stadium, with its gap between the playing area and the crowd, was dismissed as lacking atmosphere. That criticism now seems long obsolete as Odsal has come alive since the innovation of Super League. The stadium bowl is now *the* place to be for rugby enthusiasts.

It was the place to be in 1954 when after the Rugby League cup final between Halifax and Warrington had been drawn 4-4 at Wembley on the Saturday, the replayed final was at Odsal. Looking back on that first replay it is a wonder that a sports disaster didn't occur as spectators crammed into the ground. Thousands gate-crashed the event and although the official crowd was recorded at 102,567 (a world record for a Rugby League game and only recently beaten in Australia) it's well known that there were many more in the stadium as just before the kick off many spilled over onto the grass at the speedway pits end.

Attending as a ten year old with my granddad I was in the ground when the gates opened at 5.30pm two hours before the start and was at the end of the ground when Lance Todd Trophy winner Gerry Helme scored the winning try in Warrington's 8-4 win. I recall being terribly upset when I realised the programme I had bought outside wasn't the official one. Strangely enough the unofficial one I soon discarded is now worth more than the official one. The two sides met again three days later in the League Cup final and although Halifax scored the only try of the game (there had only been three tries in all three games with Warrington scoring twice at Odsal), Warrington completed a double by winning 8-7.

CRICKET

It's a well-known saying that when the white Yorkshire rose is blooming English cricket is at its strongest. Unfortunately for the Yorkshire cricketing faithful to whom cricket is more a religion than a game – despite having to come to terms with the club now playing non-Yorkshiremen – there has been little success in recent seasons. Not since the sixties has the county monopolised the county championship although at the present time there's evidence that, if Yorkshire can find playing consistency, another county championship could be in their grasp.

Yorkshire has produced hundreds of great players and many for other counties too. During the club's record history of 31 championship titles it could have fielded, if it were allowed, a second side in the championship which would have been in strong contention for the runners up spot behind Yorkshire.

A SELECTION OF YORKSHIRE'S RECORD BREAKERS AND CHARACTERS
Billy Bates – the first Englishman to achieve a Test hat-trick and first to take fourteen wickets in a Test Match
Billy Bates who, because of his fine dress sense, was known throughout his cricket career as the Duke, was a

product of that fine nursery school for Yorkshire at Lascelles Hall. An all rounder, Bates developed his slow round arm off breaks because Huddersfield kids wouldn't let him bat in street cricket as they couldn't get him out. A pro at seventeen with Rochdale, Bates made his Yorkshire debut in 1877 and toured Australia five times in the 1880s. The game, known as 'Bates Match' occurred at Melbourne in 1883. In England's 294 Bates made 55 and then took 7-28 in Australia's first innings total of 114. The hat trick and another seven-wicket haul came in the following innings. The Duke got a £31 collection for his hat trick, a colossal amount of money at the time.

Bates's singing voice was so good that on the boat ride to Australia King Kalakaua of the Sandwich Islands had him in his cabin every morning to sing 'Bonny Yorkshire Lass'. On his last tour Billy was struck on the eye by a ball in the nets and his sight impaired. Sent home, depression set in and Bates made a failed suicide attempt on the return trip. He was able to return to league cricket but died aged only 44 in 1900.

In 15 tests Bates scored 656 runs and took 50 wickets (average 16.42). For Yorkshire he took 660 wickets (average 16.70) and scored 6877 runs (8 centuries). Highest score was 136 against Sussex in 1886.

Robert Peel

Yorkshire's 100-year-old, slow, left arm bowler tradition started with Ted Peate who was joined in the team and later replaced by Bobby Peel whose liking for a drink brought a premature end to a brilliant but controversial career. Bobby, who was born in Churwell, made his debut for the white rose in 1882 and came to the fore when the club's influential cricket captain Lord Hawke

Players would cover up for Bobby's drinking when the disciplinarian Lord Hawke was on the prowl.

sacked Peate. Peel soon developed the ability to hold back the ball in flight and bowl a masterful length, and his ball was as quick as the seamers. Between 1888 and 1897 Bobby took 1273 wickets, performed the double and made 20 appearances for England taking 102 wickets. Peel's fame was so great that the illustrious actor and director Henry Ainley regarded the highlight of his life was carrying Peel's bag from the railway station to the ground. Bobby's 210 not out in Yorkshire's record score of 887 in 1896 against Warwickshire was at the time considered the best-ever innings from a left hander. His best Yorkshire return was 14-33 against Notts who were dismissed for 24 and 58 in 1888, with his England top figures being 12-69 in 1888.

One of England's great jokers he caused uproar on a

voyage to Australia when he cut sleeping hammocks and locked one of his adversaries in the boiler house until he nearly cooked. Players would cover up for Bobby's drinking when the disciplinarian Lord Hawke was on the prowl. At Sydney in 1894, England following on had set Australia 177 to win. At 113-2 overnight, during which it rained, the match looked lost and Bobby had a session. Arriving at the ground worse for wear Bobby issued his immortal words 'I'll get the buggers out before lunch' and he did with two balls to spare for 166 claiming 6-67. But the players couldn't save him from Hawke on another occasion. Covering up for him they told the Yorkshire captain that Peel was ill and Hawke replaced him. However, Peel followed his team mates out making 12 on the field. Hawke delivered his sacking after Peel reportedly urinated on the field and, trying to show he could bowl, faced the wrong way and bowled at the sightscreen instead of the wicket.

Robert Peel's career record was 9322 runs and 1311 wickets at an average of 15.74.

Wilfred Rhodes – the first bowler to take 100 wickets against Australia. Oldest Test cricketer at 52

A slow left armer following in the Yorkshire tradition whose dour classic phrase 'We don't play cricket for fun in Yorkshire' became the unwritten motto of the famous club. Wilfred Rhodes uniquely links up the two great batsmen of the 19th and 20th centuries, for in a 32-year career (his 58 games for England spanned 30 years) he bowled at the legendary master W G Grace and the Australian maestro Don Bradman. Like his great contemporary George Hirst, Rhodes was a Kirkheaton lad and the pair once shared ten wickets when Slaithwaite were skittled for nine runs (including 4 byes).

Rhodes worked in a railway yard and after finishing work on a Saturday at 2pm ran the three miles to make a 2.30pm start with Kirkheaton – until he was caught sneaking out early and got sacked. Rhodes wasn't worried. He went to Scotland to become a cricket pro. After being rejected by Warwickshire he got the chance to join Yorkshire. The story was that Yorkshire couldn't decide between him and Albert Cordingley and Wilf got the nod on the toss of a coin. A good toss to win for before Rhodes called time on his career he had amassed 16 doubles (100 runs and 100 wickets in a season). He took 100 wickets in a season 23 times and three times landed over 200. By his second season in first class cricket Rhodes was in the 1898 England team.

His best performance came at Edgbaston when he took 7-17 as Australia was put out for 36. In 1902 at the Oval he played his part in one of the greatest test matches of all time. Set 263 to beat the Australian's, England slumped to 48-5 before a spirited recovery – including a hurricane century by Gilbert Jessup – saw England need 15 to win with Hirst and Rhodes at the wicket. The story always goes that the pair agreed to get them in singles – which they did. Both players refuted this later in life on a BBC tape recording but still the story circulates in books. It is well documented that Wilfred was Yorkshire's unofficial captain on the field as the club's amateur captain often sought his opinions. The immaculately accurate bowler who never dipped in length was recalled to play for England at 49 (His last game was at 52). Rhodes worked his way up the batting order from number eleven to open with Jack Hobbs for England and held records for first and last wicket partnerships.

Career record 31,098, (average 30.04) 3597 wickets (average 16.02)

Emmott Robinson

Although he wasn't a star in test match terms, there was no bigger hero for the Yorkshire cricket enthusiast during the twenties than Emmott Robinson. The crowds loved a fighter and appreciated the little man's wholehearted team contribution in what was a successful period for the county.

The doyen of cricket writers, Neville Cardus, was a fan of Robinson's cricket and in his coverage of Roses matches made Emmott so popular in the press that when his career eventually finished Emmott was asked to write his own pieces.

Robinson hailed from Keighley and such was the rich vein of talent that for many years he struggled to make the side – not through inability but because the production line from the local league was so good. He came into the side aged 36 in 1919 and with youngsters like Herbert Sutcliffe and Percy Holmes and veterans George Hirst and Wilfred Rhodes he won a championship title in his first season. A useful swing bowler who at times opened his side's attack, Emmott could be relied on to get a few runs in Yorkshire's middle order batting. Like a later Brian Close he took on the silliest of mid on positions and when batsmen complained they got 'get on wi' thee laiking'. He had few equals as a team man. Youngsters in the crowd would mimic his eccentricities – from the dog kick at the start of his bowling run up to his bandy legged peculiar walk.

Robinson's best bowling came in the 1920 Roses' match at Bradford. Lancashire needed 52 to win with 6 wickets left. Robinson took the lot and in a Lancashire total 22 short Emmott's figures were 9-36. He liked Bradford and a couple of other great returns at the ground were 7-25 against Hants 1930 and 7-73 against

Hants in 1928. After he retired in 1931 aged 47 Yorkshire needed a 12th man and Robinson took the field again in 1933. Emmott couldn't resist an appeal, which didn't go down well with the umpire who told him 'It's got nowt to do with thee Emmott, tha's not playing'. Emmott was still around for a few years, coaching and umpiring including a spell back at Yorkshire helping the younger players.

Emmott's career record: 9,444 runs (average 24-53) 892 wickets (average 21.98)

Arthur Wood – England's oldest Test debutant

Yorkshire has had its fair share of wits none more than Arthur Wood, the stocky wicket-keeper who answered a call to play in the final 1938 test at the Oval against the Australians. The 40-year-old made his England debut in what turned out to be one of the most memorable matches of all time as England scored over 900 and fellow Yorkshireman Len Hutton passed Don Bradman's world test record. The first Yorkshire stumper to pass a thousand runs in a season, Arthur (whose cricket started at Eccleshill) took the place of Arthur Dolphin in the Yorkshire side when Dolphin had decided to don the umpire's coat.

In that historic match Wood strolled out to bat at 776-6 and his statement about being the man for the crisis has become more famous than the 53 he hit in a partnership of 100 in 90 minutes as England broke all batting records. Arthur's career lasted from 1927 to 1946 and he kept wickets in 225 consecutive matches for the county, a record that was broken later by Jimmy Binks. His other classic remark came when spinner Hedley Verity was being hit all over the field by a South African at Bradford. 'You've got him in two minds

Hedley,' he said. 'He doesn't know whether to hit you for four or six'.

Arthur's career record was 8579 runs.

Johnny Wardle

Whilst Len Shackleton was known as the Crown Prince of Football, during the 1950s Johnny Wardle was the cricket equivalent. Like Freddie Trueman – the man who succeeded him as the crowd's favourite at Yorkshire – Johnny came from a mining background working as a fitter at Hickleton Main before signing for Yorkshire. After Hedley Verity had died during the war and with his successor Arthur Booth coming to the end of his career, there was a vacancy for a left arm spinner and Johnny Wardle fitted the bill. Wardle, who was more than your average spin bowler, cultivated the Chinaman (not the one in the local takeaway, a Chinaman was a ball that turned from leg to off) and the googly (no, not what you might think but a ball that was disguised as an offbreak but turned the other way).

Fiercely competitive, Johnny didn't suffer fools gladly and woe betide anyone who dropped a catch off his bowling. The crowd loved his every turn. Whether he was pretending to do a silly misfield or running down the wicket trying to hit a six, Wardle was the people's hero. Johnny played at the same time as Tony Lock and the pair shared the duty of England's left arm spinner, otherwise his hundred test wickets would have been much greater. He was a better batter than given credit for, because he often went in when there was a need to throw the bat.

Johnny's career came to a sensational end when Yorkshire sacked him in 1959. The two parties made up before Johnny's death in 1985 after he had helped spin bowler Geoff Cope with his action. Johnny accepted an assistant coach position with Yorkshire but sadly died before becoming involved.

5750 runs (average 15.94) 1539 wickets (average 18.13)

Freddie Trueman – the first bowler to take 300 Test wickets

Has there ever been a finer sight on a cricket field than 'Fiery Fred' running in to bowl? The pigeon-toed walk back to his mark, the continued folding of his shirt sleeves, the rubbing of the ball on his thigh, black hair flying over his face, a scowl and a broad Yorkshire utterance for the batsman were the Fred Trueman trademarks that once made Prime Minister Harold Wilson describe the fast bowler as 'the greatest living Yorkshireman'.

Son of a miner from Stainton, South Yorkshire, Fred hadn't even had a game with the Colts when he made his Yorkshire debut against Cambridge University in 1949. The following year he made a test trial at Park Avenue and in 1952 he rocked India on his test debut at Headingley with a four wicket for no run start. He took 29 wickets in the four test series including 8-31 at Old Trafford. After a disappointing tour of the West Indies Freddie returned with a vengeance becoming a cricket idol whom many rate as England's best-ever fast bowler. Forging a great partnership with the ever-accurate Brian Statham, Fred played 67 matches in 13 years and took 307 wickets becoming the first bowler to pass the 300 mark. Fred answered the question would anybody equal his record with the retort, in typical Trueman bluntness: 'I don't know if they will but if they do, they'll be bloody tired'.

In 1960 Freddie shook Australia with a 5-0 spell and

at 32 in 1963 he took 34 series wickets against a very good West Indian side. A useful batsman he hit two centuries for Yorkshire and always bragged of the one he got for England (it was actually for England against Young England at the Scarborough Festival) and was a brilliant close to the wicket fielder. His popularity never waned and the cricket idol became a media personality. Even today, 30 years after his retirement, he's still up there as England's best-known cricketer.

6852 runs (average 15.15) wickets 1745 (average 17.13)

Phil Sharpe

Fielding in the slips was at one time a hiding place for one or two of the rounded bellies of cricket. A slip specialist can be an important cog in a side and during the spell from the late 1950s to the early 1970s Yorkshire had one of the best cricket has ever seen in Phil Sharpe. His 616 catches for the club played a big part in the side's last run of championship success.

It looked at one time as if Sharpe might be groomed for the Yorkshire captaincy until amateur players became a facet of the past and the club promoted its senior profession to the job. 'Chunky' (an earlier nickname for Sharpe) came to the fore when he made 1000 runs for Worksop College. Capped by Yorkshire in 1960, Phil's wintertime sport was hockey in which he also reached county standard. 2252 runs and 71 catches in 1962 brought him to the attention of the England selectors and his 12 tests saw him with an average of 46.23 much better than a list of England's later stars.

A favourite Phil Sharpe story concerns the time when an edged shot flew quickly into the slips. The batsman presumed the ball was on the way to the boundary when he saw Phil looking to give chase. The ball had, in fact, sped fast to Sharpe and his nimble reaction had seen him put the ball in his pocket. With the batsman stranded in mid wicket Sharpe coolly stopped and lobbed the ball back to stumper Jimmy Binks.

Scoring a 1000 runs in a season twelve times with a highest score of 203, Sharpe had a couple of seasons with Derbyshire before returning to Bradford where, along with his old funster from the Yorkshire dressing room, Don Wilson, he helped establish Manningham Mills in the Bradford League.

Career average 17,685 runs (average 29.72)

BOXING

Like many boxing enthusiasts I long for the 'days of yore' when there were only eight world champions and you could easily name them all. I would think even the staunchest boxing fan would struggle to name them all today, allowing for the fact we now have six different world title organisations and weights in between the eight original divisions making a total of over seventy available championships. We now have international titles which are like a stepping stone to a world title fight. Even in Britain it seems we can't put on a boxing show without a title fight and a recent innovation is British Masters Championships.

A look through boxing history has seen the sport evolve through the prize fighting era, the music hall (where the once outlawed sport found an early home), the boom in the sport prior to the first world war, the thirties gym club era, a dwindling of the small hall promotion in the 1950s to revived interest in the members' sporting club.

YORKSHIRE BOXING HEROES
'Iron' Hague
Yorkshire's first British champion was Mexborough's William 'Iron' Hague who won the heavyweight title in 1909. Hague developed his strong-boy reputation at school: insensible to pain he had a reputation for punch-

Insensible to pain, Hague had a reputation for punching brick walls.

ing brick walls. By 15 he was holding his own in booths and because his hobby was eating he soon shot up to fourteen stones. A win over Frank Craig, the Harlem Coffee Cooler, brought him to the attention of London promoters and when he got his chance to fight for the British title he saw off the champion Gunner Moir in one round. Being champion meant more 'beer and skittles' and sadly Hague neglected his training losing his title to Bombardier Billy Wells two years after he had won the title.

Frankie Round, who once used to box in the 12 in a ring specials (last man standing won) at the Plant Hotel in Mexborough in the 1920s, told me a tale that was very characteristic of the man. Frankie was courting Iron's daughter and on being introduced to the man who had been his schoolboy idol, was greeted by the former champion with 'They tell me you're gonna be a boxer son'. 'Yes, Mr Hague,' replied the eager-to-please Frankie. 'Do you know what a straight left is?' returned Iron. Before Frankie had even a chance to consider the question Iron showed him what a straight left was, leaving the young boxer the victim of his first knock down.

Bruce Woodcock
In many people's eyes the most popular Yorkshire boxer of all time – he has only been rivalled in recent years by Henry Cooper and Frank Bruno as the most popular British heavyweight ever.

Born in Doncaster in 1920 Bruce was appearing in the ring as early as six as part of a duo 'The Mighty Midgets'. Once he became British champion he captured the country's imagination in a series of fights against top American's like Lee Savold, Joe Baski, Tami Mauricillo and Lee Omah. The fights were always broadcast live with Eamonn Andrews' commentary and Barrington Dalby's summaries on radio. Bruce always ended his interview with a request for his wife to put the kettle on – he was coming home. The fights made the reputation of promoter Jack Solomans and up to 60,000 at White City witnessed the action when he fought Lee Savold. The fight was billed for the world title though it was only recognised here and in parts of Europe. Bruce was beaten by Savold who later lost to Joe Louis.

Richard Dunn
Before 1975 Richard Dunn's career had been a series of

ups and downs. Suffering from the despair of getting nowhere in the sport he made a phone call to veteran manager George Biddles. The Bradford boxer became inspired by Biddles and within a year he had won both British and European heavyweight titles and went on to fight for the greatest prize in sport against a man considered by many to be the best boxer of all time. Dunn fought Muhammad Ali in Germany and though he was never really expected to win, he won a lot of acclaim for his bravery in his five-round defeat.

Naseem Hamed
Yorkshire has its own prince of the boxing ring in Sheffield fighting machine Naseem Hamed. Within two and a half years of turning professional, Hamed had won the European bantamweight title and the WBC International Super Bantam title and in Cardiff in September 1995 he became WBO featherweight champion, a title he has carried into the new century.

THE GREATEST SPORTSMAN

The Great Wilson – 'The Man in Black'
Sherlock Holmes maybe acknowledged as the most famous man who never lived. No doubt the greatest sportsman with the same tag is the 'Great Wilson' who lived a hermit-like existence on the fictitious Ambleside Moor in remotest Yorkshire. During the 1940s and 1950s the amazing Wilson was the hero of thousands of schoolboys for whom Tuesdays couldn't come around quick enough so they could catch up with the great athlete's latest feats in the *Wizard* comic.

Wilson first surfaced in 1938 when he gatecrashed a

Wilson, who ran in bare feet, destroyed the opposition ...

half-mile race at Stamford Bridge. Despite giving the international field an extended start, Wilson, who ran in bare feet, destroyed the opposition. He was able to beat every record at every conceivable distance and field events too were a speciality. Wilson was befriended by a newspaperman called Webb, and when the great champion started to quote athletic feats going back to the eighteenth century, Webb was able to prove to himself that Wilson was approaching 300 years old. Wilson's elixir of life was contained in his secret habitation on the moor where he lived on wild plants and herbs. He wore the most meagre of clothing – a black one-piece – and never donned shoes, even in the harshest winters.

In later stories he disappeared in the Battle of Britain whilst serving in the RAF only to surface in a German prisoner-of-war camp. In 1955 Wilson turned to cricket and in the main story that summer 'The Year of the Shattered Stumps' Wilson's bowling broke bats and sidescreens as well as wickets. He dismissed the Australians to win the Ashes, the occasion being the only time Australia were all out for a single figure.

In the 1980s, a new generation was able to learn of Wilson's feats when the stories were re-hashed for the umpteenth time, and the remarkable thing was that at almost 300 he could beat his own times of years ago!